Is Lying Ever OK?

John "Cleve" Stafford

Published by John "Cleve" Stafford, 2024.

IS LYING EVER OK?

First edition. July 14, 2024.

ISBN: 979-8990054479

Written by John "Cleve" Stafford.

Also by John "Cleve" Stafford

1st Book of Devotionals
2nd Book of Devotionals
3rd Book of Devotionals
Is Lying Ever OK?

Introduction

We all lie. Anyone who says they don't lie is lying. We may try not to and may be successful a lot of the time, but we are sinners, and every now and then, we all tell an untruth. We lie about our age, our finances, our education, our history, and a plethora of other things. Someone told me recently that a study done by the University of Massachusetts concluded that 60% of adults tell a lie at least once in a ten-minute conversation. It is undoubtedly the most common of all sins, and to say we do not is foolish and contradicts the Bible. You absolutely will be a victim and perpetrator of lies. **1 John 1:8**, "*If we say we have no sin, we deceive ourselves, and the truth is not in us*" (ESV).

Lying is the perfect weapon of the Devil. He uses them expertly to try and destroy the perpetrator and the victim(s). He is a master strategist who uses this weakness present in every person on earth to disrupt relationships and cause as much mayhem as possible. As you read this book, keep this thought in your mind. Actually, it is probably a good thought to have every day. The first goal of Satan is to prevent you from discovering the freedom and peace of a personal relationship with Christ. Using the media, school, friends, and even family, he employs all sorts of lies to try and convince you there is no God. When that fails, he does not consider himself defeated. In fact, he will intensify his efforts to cause doubt to arise in your mind.

Thinking that becoming a Christian insulates you from his attacks is nothing short of delusional and can be dangerous to your spiritual journey and even your salvation. His primary motive in every despicable thing he does (which is everything he does) is to upset God's plan for your life. He wants nothing more than to remove you from the loving arms of God. The more distance he can put between you and your Creator, the more successful he will be, and lies are a brilliant way to accomplish that. Initially, you may be consumed by guilt and not feel worthy of God's love and grace, causing you to stumble even further in your faith.

But, over time, if you do not repent and return to a state of righteousness, you risk forsaking your salvation altogether as you become a habitual or pathological liar. No one can deny the destructive nature of lies. They range from "white" lies, which are considered innocent, to ones that are so huge that they literally change the course of history. This book is not an exhaustive study of every lie in the Bible but rather a brief look at some of the major ones and their effects. It is also not intended for scholars but rather for people who do not want to read and study dissertation-length material with enormous amounts of confusing information. They are my thoughts put into the simplest form I could to make them readable to the broadest audience.

I have studied the writings of several scholars and could not help noticing that many skirt the question of "Is lying ever okay?" by being vague and beating around the bush. I will not do that; at the end of the book, I will give a definitive answer.

Table of Contents

Chapter 1
What Sin Is

To fully comprehend lying and its consequences, we must first understand sin and what God thinks of it. Sin is typically understood as any thought, word, deed, or desire that goes against God's will. It includes actions that harm others, disobedience to God's commands, and attitudes such as pride, greed, and envy. Let's briefly examine what the Bible has to say about it. For a definition, we can turn to **1 John 3:4**: *"Everyone who makes a practice of sinning also practices lawlessness; sin is lawlessness."* This verse emphasizes that it is not merely a mistake or moral failing but a violation of God's authority and will. Habitual sinning is a reflection of a deeper attitude of lawlessness, which is, by definition, a disregard for God's standards.

The Bible also clearly states that we are all sinners. **Romans 3:23**, *"for all have sinned and fall short of the glory of God...."* Like you, I have encountered people who act like they do not sin. They are judgmental and quick to attack the actions of others who fall short of God's glory, but they cannot, for whatever reason, see themselves in the same light. Unfortunately for them, that attitude will endanger their salvation if left unchecked. God's attitude to sin is predictably not good. He does not sin and does not condone it ever. In fact, the concept that God cannot sin is fundamental to Christianity, based on the understanding that His nature is perfect and holy, righteous, and incapable of wrongdoing. **Psalm 92:15** says this about God, *"...to declare that the Lord is upright; he is my rock, and there is no unrighteousness in him."*

Chapter 2
Sin and God

Let me begin with a quote from the last chapter: "The concept that God cannot sin is fundamental to Christianity, based on the understanding that His nature is perfect and holy, righteous, and incapable of wrongdoing." We could say an "Amen" and move on, but let's discover what the Bible teaches about sin and God using lying as an example. In a later chapter, this question will be answered with the consequences of Adam and Eve's disobedience, but for now, let's look at **Numbers 23:19**, "*God is not man, that he should lie, or a son of man, that he should change his mind. Has he said, and will he not do it? Or has he spoken, and will he not fulfill it?*" A lot is said here, but suffice it for our context to point to the first eight words, "*God is not man, that He should lie....*" Man is fickle and can lie; God is not and does not.

Imagine the problems we would face if the Creator of the entire universe could lie. By definition, nothing in the Bible would then be considered absolute truth. Verses like **2 Timothy 3:16** would be meaningless if He told a single lie: "*All Scripture is breathed out by God and profitable for teaching, for reproof, for correction, and for training in righteousness.*" Thankfully, He is incapable of being untruthful, which establishes Him as the perfect moral standard. That is precisely why our entire moral and ethical code is based on His holiness and His Word. It is our compass because it, without exception, points toward absolute truth.

We see a similar idea proclaimed in **Numbers 23:19** and **Hebrews 6:18**: "*...so that by two unchangeable things, in which it is impossible for God to lie....*" Not only does it underscore the fact that He is incapable of lying, but it also speaks of His truthfulness and faithfulness. Let's read one more scripture that speaks of His inability to be untruthful. **Titus 1:2**, "*...in hope of eternal life, which God, who never lies, promised before* *the ages began."* By the way, the consequence of being incapable of lying means that His promises to us are set in stone, so to speak.

Now is a good time to mention that God despises lies and liars. I suppose that is self-evident from the above, but numerous scriptures witness to that fact. It is one of the Ten Commandments: **Exodus 20:16**, *"You shall not bear false witness against your neighbor."* Proverbs lists lying as one of the seven things He despises: **Proverb 6:16-19,**

> *There are six things that the Lord hates, seven that are an abomination to him:* [17.] *haughty eyes, a lying tongue, and hands that shed innocent blood,* [18.] *a heart that devises wicked plans, feet that make haste to run to evil,* [19.] *a false witness who breathes out lies, and one who sows discord among brothers.*

Okay, so God cannot sin, but what does He think of our sin? I could quote several scriptures, but I think the following one is particularly clear: **Romans 6:23**, *"For the wages of sin is death."*

Chapter 3
Why Did God Allow Sin?

Many people have wondered why God would allow sin into the world. I am sure we all think that if He disallowed it, the world would be much better and more peaceful. Think of all the wars, strife, broken relationships, pain, and suffering that could be avoided. There would be no misogyny, racism, bigotry, idolatry, adultery, lying etc., etc. So why would the omniscient (all-knowing) God purposely allow sin to enter the world when He knew the horrific consequences it would bring? To answer that question satisfactorily, we must admit something first. We are limited in our knowledge and cannot begin to fathom the unlimited mind of God.

We are told as much in **Isaiah 55:8-9**,

> For my thoughts are not your thoughts, neither are your ways my ways, declares the Lord. *9.* For as the heavens are higher than the earth, so are my ways higher than your ways and my thoughts than your thoughts.

Clearly, His mind is beyond our grasp, so the answers we give to many of life's perplexing questions have to be understood in that context. Moreover, we believe that nothing God does is for no reason. Everything has a divine intention and purpose. We may have limited mortal knowledge and understanding to contend with, but we are not totally in the dark regarding His reasoning. Careful and deliberate study of the scriptures will point us in the right direction. As we have previously read, God cannot sin, but there is a perfectly reasonable explanation for why He would allow sin into the world.

Many people, including noted scholars, say sin allows God to display who He really is: A God of incalculable, unconditional grace and mercy.

And while I cannot disagree with them, sometimes the argument becomes a little vague, to say the least. Some compared it to marriage. They said that a man or woman who has committed adultery and proceeded to ask forgiveness will experience a more profound love than even on their wedding day. That analogy falls short in so many ways, the least of which is not that it almost advocates for adultery to experience a more profound love for your spouse.

If I desire to love my wife as much as I possibly can, does it take adultery to realize it? Of course not. I can ask the same question about sin and my relationship with God, and the answer is found in **Romans 6:1-2**: "*What shall we say then? Are we to continue in sin that grace may abound?* [2.] *By no means! How can we who died to sin still live in it?*" My answer to the question will undoubtedly upset some people, but I stand by what I am about to state. There is no single reason for sin. It is not only to illustrate the glory of God but also because it is a prerequisite to having free will. God created us with the ability to choose our own destiny.

Faith in God without choice would be robotic. Free will exposes our true and deepest desire to be a child of God or to reject Him altogether. God wants a people who want to spend eternity with Him, not robots who have no choice. Of course, He wants us all to be saved; the scripture is clear about that in passages like **2 Peter 3:9**, "*The Lord is not slow to fulfill his promise as some count slowness, but is patient toward you, not wishing that any should perish, but that all should reach repentance.*" But He also wants us to decide for ourselves if that loving relationship is something we desire. Giving us free will and allowing sin sets the stage for our decision. The existence of sin helps me prove the level of my faith.

Chapter 4
The Very First Sin

When we think of the first sin, we naturally think of Adam and Eve, and technically, that is true when you consider human sin. But remove us from the picture, and suddenly, you discover that there was a previous sin. It was, of course, the rebellion of Satan. There are two main passages that speak of it, so let's read them. **Isaiah 14:12-15**,

> *How you are fallen from heaven, O Day Star, son of Dawn! How you are cut down to the ground, you who laid the nations low!* 13. *You said in your heart, 'I will ascend to heaven; above the stars of God I will set my throne on high; I will sit on the mount of assembly in the far reaches of the north;* 14. *I will ascend above the heights of the clouds; I will make myself like the Most High.'* 15. *But you are brought down to Sheol, to the far reaches of the pit.*

The other is **Ezekiel 28:12-17**,

> *Son of man, raise a lamentation over the king of Tyre, and say to him, Thus says the Lord God: 'You were the signet of perfection, full of wisdom and perfect in beauty.* 13. *You were in Eden, the garden of God; every precious stone was your covering, sardius, topaz, and diamond, beryl, onyx, and jasper, sapphire, emerald, and carbuncle; and crafted in gold were your settings and your engravings. On the day that you were created they were prepared.* 14. *You were an anointed guardian cherub. I placed you; you were on the holy mountain of God; in the midst of the stones of fire you walked.* 15. *You were blameless in your ways*

from the day you were created, till unrighteousness was found in you.

16. In the abundance of your trade you were filled with violence in your midst, and you sinned; so I cast you as a profane thing from the mountain of God, and I destroyed you, O guardian cherub, from the midst of the stones of fire. 17. Your heart was proud because of your beauty; you corrupted your wisdom for the sake of your splendor. I cast you to the ground; I exposed you before kings, to feast their eyes on you.'

There is actually a third one as well, found in the New Testament, specifically the book of **Revelation 12:7-9**,

Now war arose in heaven, Michael and his angels fighting against the dragon. And the dragon and his angels fought back, 8. but he was defeated, and there was no longer any place for them in heaven.

9. And the great dragon was thrown down, that ancient serpent, who is called the Devil and Satan, the deceiver of the whole world—he was thrown down to the earth, and his angels were thrown down with him.

The Devil sought to exalt himself above God and paid the price for his petulance. This does not prove that sin existed eternally, but rather that it came about when created beings turned against their Creator. The three previous passages prove that the sin of Satan preceded that of man. And for those who say God did not create Satan, we have a passage that proves He did. **Colossians 1:16**, "*For by him all things were created, in heaven and on earth, visible and invisible, whether thrones or dominions or* *rulers or authorities—all things were created through him and for him."* No wonder Jesus called him a murderer and liar in **John 8:44**.

Chapter 5
The First Lie

The following statement may be obvious, but "lying is not a recent invention." No one sat at a desk and thought, "I wonder what would happen if I told an untruth today?" and then went out and did so. They didn't lie and suddenly discover the power they had uncovered. No, man may have invented a lot of evil things like bombs, etc., but lying was not one of them. So when was the first lie spoken, and who can be credited for it? Well, that distinction belongs to the Devil, who introduced this foreign concept to the innocent and naïve Eve and Adam, respectively.

Genesis 3:1-4,

> *Now the serpent was more crafty than any other beast of the field that the Lord God had made. He said to the woman, "Did God actually say, 'You shall not eat of any tree in the garden'?"* [2.] *And the woman said to the serpent, "We may eat of the fruit of the trees in the garden,* [3.] *but God said, 'You shall not eat of the fruit of the tree that is in the midst of the garden, neither shall you touch it, lest you die.'"* [4.] *But the serpent said to the woman, "You will not surely die."*

The Devil had no idea the woman would fall into his trap, but I suspect a smile came over his face when he realized she did.

There are so many questions. Where the Devil came from and why he was in the garden are just two, but suffice it to say he was an angel, and his pride was his downfall. We are never told why he was in the garden, but I think it is safe to assume he went there with the specific goal of corrupting Adam and Eve. One fact that is often overlooked when the original sin is studied is how it began. The lie was introduced after doubt.

IS LYING EVER OK?

In verse one, the serpent asks, "*Did God actually say, 'You shall not eat of any tree in the garden'?*" His questioning of God would force her to think differently than she was used to, making her more susceptible to the untruth that was to follow.

Jesus labeled Satan for his nefarious intentions and also admonished those who acted like him. **John 8:44**,

> *You are of your father the Devil, and your will is to do your father's desires. He was a murderer from the beginning, and does not stand in the truth, because there is no truth in him. When he lies, he speaks out of his own character, for he is a liar and the father of lies.*

People often say the Devil must be happy when we act like him and not God, but I am not sure he knows how to be happy. I think it is instead a case of "misery loves company."

There is a Television program that aired a few years back that was called "Lucifer." It told of the Devil coming to earth and not only acting kindly to some people but also protecting them and even solving crimes. The father of lies struck yet again, making the weak portray him as an unfortunate being who was unjustly treated by God. And unfortunately, some people fell into the sympathy trap. When we are not fully aware of his evil, manipulative ploys, we run the risk of being devoured. **1 Peter 5:8**, "*Be sober-minded; be watchful. Your adversary the Devil prowls around like a roaring lion, seeking someone to devour.*" Always, always remember, he is the father of lies, so do not be sucked into them. Do not let your guard down for one second because he is watching for the tiniest lapse in your attention to pounce.

Chapter 6
Lying Scriptures

Although not all of these verses apply to the book's content, I thought I would add them anyway.

<u>LIAR</u>

Proverbs 19:22, "*What is desired in a man is steadfast love, and a poor man is better than a liar.*"

John 8:44, "*You are of your father the Devil, and your will is to do your father's desires. He was a murderer from the beginning, and does not stand in the truth, because there is no truth in him. When he lies, he speaks out of his own character, for he is a liar and the father of lies.*"

Romans 3:4, "*By no means! Let God be true though every one were a liar, as it is written, 'That you may be justified in your words, and prevail when you are judged.'*"

1 John 1:10, "*If we say we have not sinned, we make him a liar, and his word is not in us.*"

1 John 4:20, "*If anyone says, 'I love God,' and hates his brother, he is a liar; for he who does not love his brother whom he has seen cannot love God whom he has not seen.*"

IS LYING EVER OK?

LIARS

1 Titus 4:2, "*through the insincerity of liars whose consciences are seared...*"

Revelation 21:8, "*But as for the cowardly, the faithless, the detestable, as for murderers, the sexually immoral, sorcerers, idolaters, and all liars, their portion will be in the lake that burns with fire and sulfur, which is the second death.*"

LIE

Leviticus 19:11, "*You shall not steal; you shall not deal falsely; you shall not lie to one another.*"

Numbers 23:19, "*God is not man, that he should lie, or a son of man, that he should change his mind. Has he said, and will he not do it? Or has he spoken, and will he not fulfill it?*"

Proverbs 14:5, "*A faithful witness does not lie, but a false witness breathes out lies.*"

Acts 5:3, "*But Peter said, 'Ananias, why has Satan filled your heart to lie to the Holy Spirit and to keep back for yourself part of the proceeds of the land?'*"

Romans 1:25, "*because they exchanged the truth about God for a lie and worshiped and served the creature rather than the Creator, who is blessed forever! Amen.*"

Colossians 3:9, "*Do not lie to one another, seeing that you have put off the old self with its practices.*"

Hebrews 6:18, "*so that by two unchangeable things, in which it is impossible for God to lie, we who have fled for refuge might have strong encouragement to hold fast to the hope set before us.*"

1 John 2:21, "*I write to you, not because you do not know the truth, but because you know it, and because no lie is of the truth.*"

LIES

Psalms 101:7, "*No one who practices deceit shall dwell in my house; no one who utters lies shall continue before my eyes.*"

Proverbs 19:5, "*A false witness will not go unpunished, and he who breathes out lies will not escape.*"

Titus 1:2, "*in hope of eternal life, which God, who never lies, promised before the ages began.*"

<u>LYING</u>

Proverbs 12:22, "*Lying lips are an abomination to the Lord, but those who act faithfully are his delight.*"

Proverbs 26:28, "*A lying tongue hates its victims, and a flattering mouth works ruin.*"

Hosea 4:2, "*there is swearing, lying, murder, stealing, and committing adultery; they break all bounds, and bloodshed follows bloodshed.*"

Chapter 7

The Consequences of the First Lie

The consequences of the first lie began way before Adam and Eve. When Satan and his followers were cast out of heaven, the foundation was laid for it. Now, to be clear, the consequences did not result from the lie but rather from the actions of Adam and Eve, who believed it. I am not trying to downplay their part in it because their actions obviously led to it, but I want to clarify that it was the first lie that ultimately led to God's wrath. I can say without any reservations that there has never been a sin with more severe or far-reaching consequences. As the saying goes, "It was one for the record books."

Spiritual Separation from God

The most immediate consequence of their disobedience was a spiritual separation from God. The bliss of an existence without the slightest bit of concern was destroyed by the manipulation of the Devil and the weakness of Adam and Eve. Unfortunately for us, this separation caused a landslide of other consequences.

Physical Death

Man would lose the privilege of living forever – at least here on earth. **Genesis 2:17**, "*but of the tree of the knowledge of good and evil you shall not eat, for in the day that you eat of it you shall surely die.*" We went from no decay or mortality to a life that "winds down" to our deathbed, with decay accompanying it as a reminder of our mortality.

And, by the way, we dragged the animals into that future with us. The serpent was justly condemned, but no other animal was part of the fall of man, yet they would have to suffer the same fate. But, let it be known that the righteousness of God is such that we will all live eternally outside of this mortal body. Yes, we are destined to suffer physical death, but whether or not we suffer a spiritual one is up to us. We are faced with a choice in our lives that is ours by virtue of free will gifted to us by

God. Our decision to accept or reject the gospel of Christ will determine where we spend our forever.

Sin Nature

As a result of Adam and Eve's disobedience, the concept of a "sin nature" was introduced. Unfortunately for us, that sinful nature is universal, so thinking that we will somehow overcome it is delusional. In fact, we are told the following in **Romans 5:12**, "*Therefore, just as sin came into the world through one man, and death through sin, and so death spread to all men because all sinned.*" It is pretty clear that the natural tendency toward pride, selfishness, lying, and a plethora of other sins is something we are born with. Instead of denying our sinful nature, most of us grapple with the same conflicting ideas Paul did. **Romans 7:15**, "*For I do not understand my own actions. For I do not do what I want, but I do the very thing I hate.*" I am not excusing sinful actions any more than Paul was, but instead highlighting our innate tendency to act disobediently to God's Word – even when we know we are doing it. Suffice it to say we all sin. **Romans 3:23**, "*for all have sinned and fall short of the glory of God.*"

Cursed Ground

This next consequence meant hard labor for mankind. The previously harmonious relationship between man and nature was forever disrupted. The ground that previously only produced abundant fruit and was easy to harvest would now produce thorns, thistles, and the like, making agriculture difficult and laborious. **Genesis 3:19**, "*By the sweat of your face you shall eat bread, till you return to the ground, for out of it you were taken; for you are dust, and to dust you shall return.*" I am pretty sure every farmer who has ever had to raise a crop of some kind understands this curse all too well.

Pain in Childbirth

Genesis 3:16, "*To the woman he said, 'I will surely multiply your pain in childbearing; in pain you shall bring forth children. Your desire shall be contrary to your husband, but he shall rule over you.'*" Every man who ever stood at his wife's side while she was in the throes of childbirth knows the pain she is going through – because she will not be shy to tell him about it. I smile as I write this because my daughter informed us last night that she is pregnant, so her husband is going to find out for himself what kind of pain she will be in. Undoubtedly, the God of all creation who pronounced this curse simultaneously gave women the courage and pain threshold to endure it. The resilience of women who bear the pain of a firstborn and then decide to do it again, sometimes multiple times more, is a testament to the courage and endurance given to them by God.

Expulsion from Eden

Their disobedience resulted in their expulsion from the most beautiful place ever on this earth. What a shock it must have been to be forced to leave the perfect earthly paradise of Eden and have to deal with the difficulties beyond its borders. **Genesis 3:22-24**,

> *Then the Lord God said, 'Behold, the man has become like one of us in knowing good and evil. Now, lest he reach out his hand and take also of the tree of life and eat, and live forever—'* [23.] *therefore the Lord God sent him out from the garden of Eden to work the ground from which he was taken.* [24.] *He drove out the man, and at the east of the garden of Eden he placed the cherubim and a flaming sword that turned every way to guard the way to the tree of life.*

What a loving God we have: a God who loves us so much that despite their disobedience, He clothed them and gave them a way to deal with every curse. To the woman, He gave courage and strength to overcome the pain of childbirth. To the man, courage and power to overcome the challenges he will face in agriculture. To both sexes, the opportunity to redeem themselves by the blood of Christ on the cross. And, even though the beautiful, idyllic Garden of Eden was no longer an option, a much more beautiful place called heaven awaits those who remain obedient till death.

Chapter 8
First Lie Revisited (Gen. 3)

The serpent lies to Eve (**Gen. 3:1-4**). I will not revisit that lie because we have dealt with it in the previous chapter, but there are one or two things worth adding. Eve was deceived, but Adam was not somewhere else at the time. From the words in the passage, it seems more likely that he was present or very close by. **Genesis 3:6**,

> So when the woman saw that the tree was good for food, and that it was a delight to the eyes, and that the tree was to be desired to make one wise, she took of its fruit and ate, and she also gave some to her husband who was with her, and he ate.

Notice how it does not say she called out to him or went looking for him.

Too many men blame women for introducing sin, but God makes it clear that being deceived by the Devil's lie falls more on his shoulders than hers. In the following paragraphs, we will see that he tried to pass the blame on to Eve, but if that was his intention, it backfired spectacularly. **First Corinthians 15:21-22**, "*For as by a man came death, by a man has come also the resurrection of the dead. 22. For as in Adam all die, so also in Christ shall all be made alive.*" Not to be too lighthearted, but after the Lord confronts Adam, he does something somewhat ambiguous.

Let's read **Genesis 3:9-13** to discover what it was.

> But the Lord God called to the man and said to him, 'Where are you?' 10. And he said, 'I heard the sound of you in the garden, and I was afraid, because I was naked, and I hid myself.' 11. He said, 'Who told you that you were naked? Have you eaten of the

tree of which I commanded you not to eat?' [12.] *The man said,
'The woman whom you gave to be with me, she gave me fruit of
the tree, and I ate.'* [13.] *Then the Lord God said to the woman,
'What is this that you have done?' The woman said, 'The serpent
deceived me, and I ate.'*

Did you notice what it was? Adam says to God that the woman He
gave to him gave him the fruit, and he ate it.

Firstly, it kind of sounds like he is passive-aggressively blaming God
for giving him the woman in the first place. Now, he may just be stating
the obvious, but why tell the Creator what He did? Since sin was now
in their hearts, it is more likely that he was passing the buck, especially
when he says the woman gave it to him to eat. That is indicative of what
we would do under similar circumstances. How often have you been in
trouble at home or work and then passed the blame on to someone else?
We frequently go to great lengths to avoid taking responsibility for the
consequences of our own actions.

Chapter 9
Cain Lies about Abel (Gen. 4)

Genesis 4:1-16,

Now Adam knew Eve his wife, and she conceived and bore Cain, saying, 'I have gotten a man with the help of the Lord.' 2. And again, she bore his brother Abel. Now Abel was a keeper of sheep, and Cain a worker of the ground. 3. In the course of time Cain brought to the Lord an offering of the fruit of the ground, 4. and Abel also brought of the firstborn of his flock and of their fat portions. And the Lord had regard for Abel and his offering, 5. but for Cain and his offering he had no regard. So Cain was very angry, and his face fell. 6. The Lord said to Cain, 'Why are you angry, and why has your face fallen?

7. If you do well, will you not be accepted? And if you do not do well, sin is crouching at the door. Its desire is contrary to you, but you must rule over it.' 8. Cain spoke to Abel his brother. And when they were in the field, Cain rose up against his brother Abel and killed him. 9. <u>Then the Lord said to Cain, 'Where is Abel your brother?' He said, 'I do not know; am I my brother's keeper?'</u> 10. And the Lord said, 'What have you done? The voice of your brother's blood is crying to me from the ground. 11. And now you are cursed from the ground, which has opened its mouth to receive your brother's blood from your hand. 12. When you work the ground, it shall no longer yield to you its strength. You shall be a fugitive and a wanderer on the earth.'

13. Cain said to the Lord, 'My punishment is greater than I can bear. 14. Behold, you have driven me today away from the ground, and from your face I shall be hidden. I shall be a fugitive and a wanderer on the earth, and whoever finds me will kill me.' 15. Then the Lord said to him, 'Not so! If anyone kills Cain, vengeance shall be taken on him sevenfold.' And the Lord put a mark on Cain, lest any who found him should attack him. 16. Then Cain went away from the presence of the Lord and settled in the land of Nod, east of Eden.

We all know this story to be the first case of murder. Cain was jealous because God looked more favorably on Abel's offering, but the part of the story we are concentrating on is the underlined portion – verse 9. When God enquires about his brother's whereabouts, he lies and makes one of the most famous quotes of all time, "...*am I my brother's keeper?*" I'm not sure who he thought he was dealing with, but the God of all creation chose to ignore that ridiculous statement and accused him of murder. The consequence taking his brother's life was that he was cursed to be a restless wanderer. Furthermore, the ground would no longer yield good crops for him. That said, we want to look specifically at the lie because there is also a lesson to learn from it.

When God accuses him of murdering his brother with the words, "*What have you done?*" it witnesses to His omniscience (all-knowingness). In other words, we cannot hide anything from God. **Psalms 139:4**, "*Even before a word is on my tongue, behold, O Lord, you know it altogether.*" That's right, He already knows what we *will* say before we even say it. Then we also have **1 John 3:20**. "*For whenever our heart condemns us, God is greater than our heart, and he knows everything.*" The question we are left with is, "Why lie if He already knows the truth, and why lie to other people if we know He is everywhere and knows everything we say?"

Chapter 10
Abraham Lies to Pharaoh (Gen. 12)

Genesis 12:11-13,

> *When he was about to enter Egypt, he said to Sarai his wife,*
> *'I know that you are a woman beautiful in appearance,* [12.] *and*
> *when the Egyptians see you, they will say, "This is his wife." Then*
> *they will kill me, but they will let you live.* [13.] *Say you are my*
> *sister, that it may go well with me because of you, and that my*
> *life may be spared for your sake.'*

Most people would think Abraham's lie to Pharaoh was rather cowardly. I think it is safe to assume that most men could not imagine telling anyone their wife is their sister. But remember something: it is easy to say what you think you will do in a life-threatening situation, but it is an entirely different story when you are actually facing it.

Fear can make us do what we would typically never consider doing. Firstly, this lie stems from a lack of trust in God. Remember, this man trusted God completely when told to leave his country. **Genesis 12:1,** "*Now the Lord said to Abram, 'Go from your country and your kindred and your father's house to the land that I will show you.'*" How many of us would do that? How many of us would do that without hesitation as Abraham did? **Genesis 12:4,** "*So Abram went, as the Lord had told him, and Lot went with him. Abram was seventy-five years old when he departed from Haran.*"

Where did that trust go? I think we can be like that. Our first few years after discovering God and being baptized are all about trusting Him as much as possible. But, over time, as things happen and we suffer trials and persecution, our trust in the Almighty begins to wane. Abraham's mistrust of God caused him to lie, which damaged his relationship with Pharoah. Unfortunately, Pharoah would suffer greatly as a result of Abraham's deception. **Genesis 12:17**, "*But the Lord afflicted Pharoah and his house with great plagues because of Sarai, Abram's wife.*"

Sometimes, the innocent party pays the price for the lies. As we have seen, lies always have consequences and can be devastating, even if it is not always to the person speaking the untruth. Don't think, however, that you can lie, and someone else will always pay the price. Don't think that God has not made a note of the lie. It is better to repent and correct what you have done rather than wait to see whether God will or will not punish you for your sin.

Moreover, God will not always work things out perfectly for us as He did for Abraham and Sarah. And while we are speaking of her, the lie also belongs to her because she did not correct it before Pharaoh. She was complicit in the lie. But could it be argued that she was only obeying her husband? In the next chapter, Abraham also lies to Abimelech, and the excuse he makes when the lie is uncovered may shed light on the reason for Sarah's silence. **Genesis 20:13**, "*And when God caused me to wander from my father's house, I said to her, 'This is the kindness you must do me: at every place to which we come, say of me, 'He is my brother.'*"

Remember, scripture often portrays her as a faithful wife: **1 Pe. 3:5-6**,

> *For this is how the holy women who hoped in God used to adorn themselves, by submitting to their own husbands,* ^{6.} *as Sarah obeyed Abraham, calling him lord. And you are her children, if you do good and do not fear anything that is frightening.*

Chapter 11
Abraham lies to Abimelech (Gen. 20)

As we will discover now, the lie Abraham told Pharaoh about Sarah not being his wife happened a second time. **Genesis 20:1-2,**

> *From there Abraham journeyed toward the territory of the Negeb and lived between Kadesh and Shur; and he sojourned in Gerar.* ^{2.} *And Abraham said of Sarah, his wife, 'She is my sister.' And Abimelech, king of Gerar, sent and took Sarah.*

This time, God intervenes and comes to Abimelech in a dream, warning him to return Sarah or face serious consequences. **Genesis 20:7,** *"Now then, return the man's wife, for he is a prophet, so that he will pray for you, and you shall live. But if you do not return her, know that you shall surely die, you and all who are yours."*

Abimelech does as God instructs and even blesses the couple with sheep, oxen, male and female servants, and a thousand pieces of silver. Lies are sometimes nullified if they are discovered early enough and if we are prepared to right any wrongs that may have happened, whether we are the victim or the perpetrator. I don't want to dwell on this lie too much since it is similar to the previous one, but I do want to answer a point my wife made when speaking to her about these two lies. Many people have read **Genesis 20:12** and claim that it was technically not a lie: *"Besides, she is indeed my sister, the daughter of my father though not the daughter of my mother, and she became my wife."*

But a half-truth is still a lie. The lie was not that they were half-siblings but that they were not married. What would they have done if God had not intervened and Sarah had been "taken" by one of the men they lied to? God will not always intervene for us when we lie, so there is no guarantee we will prevent the unfortunate consequences of our lies.

That is why I said in a previous chapter, "It is better not to lie than to try and find out if God will bail us out." The chances are much greater that we will not be saved by His intervention. There is one more question, which is not the thrust of this book, that I want to address briefly. "Why did Pharaoh suffer consequences and not Abimelech?"

Some say God did this because He knew the latter would respond positively while the former would not. That may be true, but it is much safer not to assume why God does things we don't understand. Maybe one day, in the afterlife, we will be told why, but for now, we accept His actions by faith without always understanding them.

Chapter 12
Sarah Lies to God (Gen. 18)

As we shall see, this lie does not have immediate consequences that we are told of, but nevertheless, it reveals an important characteristic of God that appears many times in the Bible. Abraham has an encounter with three visitors, who are often described as angels or a theophany (appearance of God). We are not given much detail, but it appears that Abraham recognized that they were somehow extraordinary. **Genesis 18:2-3**,

> *He lifted up his eyes and looked, and behold, three men were standing in front of him. When he saw them, he ran from the tent door to meet them and bowed himself to the earth* [3.] *and said, 'O Lord, if I have found favor in your sight, do not pass by your servant.'*

He offered them water to wash their feet, instructed Sarah to make cakes from fine flour, and prepared a calf for them to eat. While they were eating, they asked where his wife was, and he answered that she was in the tent. Without any introduction, their following words were, *"The Lord said, 'I will surely return to you about this time next year, and Sarah your wife shall have a son.' And Sarah was listening at the tent door behind him"* (**Genesis 18:10**). The eavesdropping Sarah laughed to herself, questioning her ability to bear a child in her old age. This is where the lie comes into the story.

Genesis 8:13-15,

> *The Lord said to Abraham, 'Why did Sarah laugh and say, "Shall I indeed bear a child, now that I am old?"* [14.] *Is anything too hard for the Lord? At the appointed time I will return to you,*

about this time next year, and Sarah shall have a son.' But Sarah denied it, saying, 'I did not laugh,' for she was afraid. He said, 'No, but you did laugh.'

Two things stand out in these two verses. Firstly, it is the Lord who questioned Abraham, presumably through one of the men who were representing Him. Secondly, despite her dismissal of the fact, God reminds them that not only is nothing impossible for Him but also that there will be a baby boy born to her the following year.

If you recall, I said at the beginning of the chapter that there were no immediate consequences but that the episode revealed an important characteristic of God. What I was referring to is His omniscience. Sarah might have thought she was alone, but God was right there to hear her every thought. That's right, not even our thoughts can be hidden from Him. **Hebrews 4:13** witnesses that fact with these words, "*And no creature is hidden from his sight, but all are naked and exposed to the eyes of him to whom we must give account.*"

Jesus Himself also proves His oneness with the Father in **John 1:47-48**,

Jesus saw Nathanael coming toward him and said of him, 'Behold, an Israelite indeed, in whom there is no deceit!' [48.] *Nathanael said to him, 'How do you know me?' Jesus answered him, 'Before Philip called you, when you were under the fig tree, I saw you.'*

We are entirely delusional when we think we can commit a sin that God will not see. There is no place dark enough, no place deep enough, and no place so isolated that God is not there. That fact is made perfectly clear in **Jeremiah 23:24**, "*Can a man hide himself in secret places so that I cannot see him? declares the Lord. Do I not fill heaven and earth? declares the Lord.*" If only we would live our lives as if we not only know but fully believe that we are never out of His sight. How differently we would behave if we did.

Chapter 13
Jacob Lies to Isaac (Gen. 27)

The lie of Jacob has been the source of much study and consternation for many Christians. Some mistakenly believe that Jacob escaped the consequences of his deception, but a careful study of his life after the lie reveals quite the opposite. He was the younger of twin brothers born to Isaac and Rebekah and was destined for greatness. Incontrovertible evidence of the actions that would dictate his life later is already discovered before he and his brother, Esau, were born.

Genesis 25:21-23,

> *Isaac prayed to the LORD on behalf of his wife, because she was childless. The LORD answered his prayer, and his wife Rebekah became pregnant. [1] The babies jostled each other within her, and she said, 'Why is this happening to me?' So she went to inquire of the LORD. [2] The LORD said to her, 'Two nations are in your womb, and two peoples from within you will be separated; one people will be stronger than the other, and the older will serve the younger.'*

This story could be the subject of many chapters, but since the context is lying, we will only briefly deal with some of the more important points to clarify the story.

Firstly, a hidden detail in the story is sometimes questioned: why did the firstborn receive a double portion of the inheritance? Simply, according to tradition, the oldest son would have to take in any widower or unmarried sisters since they did not receive any of the inheritance. It sounds like a blessing to be the firstborn until you realize that all the

---

1. *https://www.biblestudytools.com/genesis/25-22.html*

2. *https://www.biblestudytools.com/genesis/25-23.html*

responsibility of the women in the family fell on him. Secondly, why did God not just make Jacob the firstborn? The easiest way to explain this is that He does not interfere with the natural birth order but instead chooses the best sibling to further His will.

And, for the record, Jacob was not the only younger son who was chosen over the older one(s). Isaac was chosen over Ishmael, Judah over his three older siblings, and David over no less than seven brothers. In the case of Jacob and Esau, it must be remembered that God knew their character, choosing the more noble of the two. That is evidenced in **Hebrews 12:16**, *"that no one is sexually immoral or unholy like Esau, who sold his birthright for a single meal."* Keep in mind the fact that Esau willingly sold his birthright – it was not stolen from him. After Isaac sends his oldest son to hunt game and prepare a meal for him, Rebekah overhears and devises a plan to trick Isaac.

Rebekah dresses Jacob in Esau's clothes and covers his hands and neck with goat skin to imitate Esau's hairy skin. The disguise fools his almost blind father, and he believes the lie that Jacob is Esau, bestowing on him the blessing intended for his brother. **Genesis 27:22-24**,

> *So Jacob went near to Isaac his father, who felt him and said, 'The voice is Jacob's voice, but the hands are the hands of Esau.'* *23. And he did not recognize him because his hands were hairy like his brother Esau's hands. So he blessed him.* *24. He said, 'Are you really my son Esau?' He answered, 'I am.'*

Genesis 27:28-29,

> *May God give you of the dew of heaven and of the fatness of the earth and plenty of grain and wine.* *29. Let peoples serve you, and nations bow down to you. Be lord over your brothers, and may your mother's sons bow down to you. Cursed be everyone who curses you, and blessed be everyone who blesses you!*

I suppose one could say that it was the earliest case of identity fraud, which is a particularly dangerous kind of lie. Lying by pretending to have served in the military or something like that to gain an advantage over someone else is not all that uncommon today. I trust that we would never seriously consider perpetrating that kind of lie in our lifetime, understanding the devastating consequences the victim may suffer.

Chapter 14
Sons of Jacob Lie to Him (Gen. 37)

In **Genesis 37,** we encounter the story of Joseph's being sold by his brothers. In **vs. 1-11,** we learn of the tension his dreams caused between him and his brothers. It did not help that he also brought a bad report about them to his father or that the latter made his favorite son a robe of many colors. Sibling jealousy was not new to the world, and we may recall the first time we read of the jealousy of Cain, who would murder his brother. It is one of the most destructive emotions that, as we have learned, can lead to violent outcomes. As the story of Joseph teaches us, parents who show blatant favoritism can cause all sorts of consternation within the family.

This is clearly evidenced in **Genesis 37:4,** "*But when his brothers saw that their father loved him more than all his brothers, they hated him and could not speak peacefully to him.*" As if that was not bad enough, the young teen lad had two dreams that further incited their hatred for him. In the first dream, they were binding sheaves in the field when Joseph's sheaf rose and stood upright, while their sheaves gathered around and bowed down to his sheaf (**37:5-7**). His brothers asked if he intended to reign over them, and they hated him even more for his dreams and words (**37:8**). In his second dream, the sun, moon, and eleven stars were bowing down to him (**37:9**).

He told this to his father and brothers; his father rebuked him, asking if he, his mother, and his brothers were to bow to the ground before him (**37:10**). It is not hard to imagine why they would be so angry and hateful towards him, but what happens next turns the brothers into eventual liars. In **Genesis 37:12-36** we read of their plot to kill him and blame wild animals for his death. The only reason they did not go through with their plan was because Reuben, his oldest brother, did not want to shed his blood. He suggested they throw their younger brother into a pit and leave him to die, but Reuben intended to save him later. Ultimately, he was sold to Ishmaelites for twenty shekels of silver ($165 in 2024).

Reuben was not present for the sale of his brother, and when he returned, he was so distraught that he tore his clothes. **Genesis 37:31-33,**

> *Then they took Joseph's robe and slaughtered a goat and dipped the robe in the blood. [32.] And they sent the robe of many colors and brought it to their father and said, 'This we have found; please identify whether it is your son's robe or not.' [33.] And he identified it and said, 'It is my son's robe. A fierce animal has devoured him. Joseph is without doubt torn to pieces.'*

Their lie was not a direct one, but rather one of omission. They presented the bloody robe to their father and allowed him to make an assumption based on their omission of the facts.

This type of lie is perpetrated for one or more of the following reasons: Avoiding the consequences or negative repercussions, manipulating perceptions, preserving relationships by appearing innocent of any wrongdoing, strategic reasons to gain some type of an advantage, rationalizing one's "silence" by believing the other person was the perpetrator of actions justifying the omission, or easing one's conscience. While the text does not provide a detailed account of Jacob's reaction to the full realization of his sons' deception, it is clear that he learns the truth about Joseph's survival and the earlier lie through later events.

> *And they told him, 'Joseph is still alive, and he is ruler over all the land of Egypt.' And his heart became numb, for he did not believe them. But when they told him all the words of Joseph, which he had said to them, and when he saw the wagons that*

IS LYING EVER OK?

Joseph had sent to carry him, the spirit of their father Jacob revived. And Israel said, 'It is enough; Joseph my son is still alive. I will go and see him before I die' (**Genesis 45:26-28**).

This type of lie is not only common today but is also a particularly nefarious type that has the potential to cause incalculable damage to relationships.

Chapter 15

Potiphar's Wife Lies to Him (Gen. 37)

Poor old Joseph does not seem to be able to escape from liars. After being sold to the Egyptians, he finds himself in the home of Potiphar, the captain of Pharaoh's guard, and his wife. Almost immediately, the wife tries to seduce young Joseph:

> *Now Joseph was handsome in form and appearance.* [7.] *And after a time, his master's wife cast her eyes on Joseph and said, 'Lie with me.'* [8.] *But he refused and said to his master's wife, 'Behold, because of me my master has no concern about anything in the house, and he has put everything that he has in my charge.* [9.] *He is not greater in this house than I am, nor has he kept back anything from me except you, because you are his wife. How then can I do this great wickedness and sin against God?'* (**Genesis 39:6-9**).

Potiphar's wife did not let that deter her, and she continued with her attempts until a day came when she caught him alone in the house. Grabbing onto his garment, she once again asked him to "lie with her," but again, he refused, leaving his garment in her hand and fleeing from the house. This incensed her, and she called the men of her household and accused Joseph of attempting to rape her. That lie was bad enough, but she repeated it to her husband as well in **Genesis 39:17-19**,

> *"... and she told him the same story, saying, 'The Hebrew servant, whom you have brought among us, came in to me to laugh at me.* [18.] *But as soon as I lifted up my voice and cried, he left his garment beside me and fled out of the house.'* [19.] *As soon as his*

master heard the words that his wife spoke to him, 'This is the
way your servant treated me,' his anger was kindled.'"

That lie could be classified as a false accusation and/or slander and resulted in Joseph's imprisonment. Although He was later released after interpreting the Pharaoh's dreams, he was still wrongly accused and imprisoned. There have been and still are many people who have been wrongly accused of rape or other serious crimes that are wasting away in jails all across the globe. The Bible does not reveal what punishment, if any, Potiphar's wife was subjected to for her lies, but do not be misled into thinking she may have escaped repercussions altogether. We may escape punishment on earth, but on that great Day of Judgment, our sins will catch up with us, and if unrepentant, the cost will be very dear indeed.

Chapter 16

False Witnesses Lie About Jesus (Mat. 26)

Sometimes, we are the victims of other people's lies, but it's not as if we are totally innocent and never tell a "fib" ourselves. That is not a justification for their lies, but it can sometimes be a "tit-for-tat" situation. Jesus, on the other hand, was no stranger to the lies of other people, even though He was incapable of lying Himself. We can classify the lies told about Jesus in the following ways. Firstly, there are the lies that fulfilled prophecy. Of course, all the lies fall into that category because none could possibly catch Jesus off guard. From a purely theological perspective, they fulfilled Old Testament prophecies about the suffering and rejection of the Messiah.

We clearly see that in **Isaiah 53:3-7**,

> *He was despised and rejected by men, a man of sorrows and acquainted with grief, and as one from whom men hide their faces he was despised, and we esteemed him not. 4. Surely he has borne our griefs and carried our sorrows; yet we esteemed him stricken, smitten by God, and afflicted. 5. But he was pierced for our transgressions; he was crushed for our iniquities; upon him was the chastisement that brought us peace, and with his wounds we are healed. 6. All we like sheep have gone astray; we have turned—every one—to his own way; and the Lord has laid on him the iniquity of us all. 7. He was oppressed, and he was afflicted, yet he opened not his mouth; like a lamb that is led to the slaughter, and like a sheep that before its shearers is silent, so he opened not his mouth.*

IS LYING EVER OK?

It seems incredulous to us today, given all the scripture and knowledge we possess, that anyone could speak falsehoods about the Son of Man, but we should never forget that God, in His foreknowledge, knew precisely what would happen. As sad and unfair as it may seem to us, we should also bear in mind that those lies ultimately led to His death and resurrection, and our salvation. Secondly, there are lies that could be called the "general lies." The sample scripture for this is **John 18:29-30**, "*So Pilate went outside to them and said, 'What accusation do you bring against this man?'* [30.] *They answered him, 'If this man were not doing evil, we would not have delivered him over to you.'*"

Notice how the Jewish leaders' response to Pilate was intentionally vague. They were fully aware that they had nothing to charge Him with, so instead of specifying any particular crime or accusation, they merely implied that Jesus' wrongdoing was self-evident. The lack of specificity could be seen as an attempt to pressure Pilate into an action he did not fully agree with. It further suggests that they expected Pilate to trust their judgment despite their vagueness.

Thirdly, there are legal lies because they were committed before the Sanhedrin. **Matthew 26:59-61**,

> *Now the chief priests and the whole council were seeking false testimony against Jesus that they might put him to death,* [60.] *but they found none, though many false witnesses came forward. At last two came forward* [61.] *and said, 'This man said, "I am able to destroy the temple of God, and to rebuild it in three days."'*

Although many witnesses came forward, they were not found credible – until two came forward with a specific charge. In an earlier chapter, I stated that some of the best lies are born from the truth, and this is a perfect example of that.

The two false witnesses took the words of Jesus and then misstated them so that the Sanhedrin would interpret them as a blasphemous threat to the temple. The religious leaders were not interested in a fair trial, and all they needed was some kind of a crime to charge Jesus with, something that the false witnesses delivered to them. The last type of lie I call the Pilate lies, obviously because it happened before him. The relevant scriptures **Luke 23:1-2**,

> *Then the whole company of them arose and brought him before Pilate.* [2.] *And they began to accuse him, saying, 'We found this man misleading our nation and forbidding us to give tribute to Caesar, and saying that he himself is Christ, a king'.*

John 19:12 illustrates once again the willingness of the Jewish leaders to pressure first the Sanhedrin and now the Roman authorities to find Jesus guilty: *"From then on Pilate sought to release him, but the Jews cried out, 'If you release this man, you are not Caesar's friend. Everyone who makes himself a king opposes Caesar.'"* Lies and pressure were all the Jewish leaders had, and although it was baseless, they managed to convince Pilate to go ahead and proclaim Jesus guilty as charged. Before moving on to the next chapter I want us to look at some of the reasons they were so willing to lie about the Messiah.

Firstly, Jesus was a real and present danger to the Jewish religious leaders. His teachings, popularity, and claims to be the Messiah challenged their power and the status quo, something they were willing to maintain at any cost. Secondly, there were also those who feared his popularity and teaching could lead to political unrest, which would solicit a harsh response from the Roman authorities. A third group was trying to please the Jewish leaders, and they probably felt they would not suffer any consequence for their deceitful action if it benefitted the leaders. One thing is sure – there are many reasons people lie about us, and it is seldom, if ever, for our benefit.

Chapter 17
Peter's Denial of Jesus (Mat. 26)

Yes, even the illustrious Peter, who was the only mortal to walk on water (albeit only a step or two). Some people have contended that it was not actually a lie but rather a denial, but I fail to see the difference. Saying He did not know Jesus and that he was not a disciple was nothing short of a lie. The events leading up to Peter's denial of Jesus unfold amidst the intense and foreboding atmosphere of Jesus' final hours. After celebrating the Passover meal with His disciples, Jesus leads them to the Mount of Olives, where He predicts their imminent desertion, saying, *"You will all fall away because of me this night. For it is written, 'I will strike the shepherd, and the sheep of the flock will be scattered'"* (**Matthew 26:31**).

Like most of us, Peter, who was fervent in his loyalty, vehemently denies that he would ever do such a dastardly thing. Peter: *"Though they all fall away because of you, I will never fall away"* (**Matthew 26:33**). Jesus, who is all-knowing, is not fooled by his words and replies with the following solemn prophecy, *"Truly, I tell you, this very night, before the rooster crows, you will deny me three times"* (**Matthew 26:34**). Despite this, the disciple is undeterred in his determination to prove to Jesus that he would never betray his loyalty to Him and insists, *"Even if I must die with you, I will not deny you!"* (**Matthew 26:35**). All the other disciples echo Peter's sentiment.

After the betrayal of Judas and Jesus' arrest, Peter and the other disciples immediately flee: *"... Then all the disciples left him and fled"* (**Matthew 26:56**). As we see, it took almost no time for them to go from "I will die with you!" to "I am outta here!" Peter follows the arresting party at a distance and soon faces the chilling fulfillment of Jesus' prophecy. **Matthew 26:69-75**,

Now Peter was sitting outside in the courtyard. And a servant girl came up to him and said, 'You also were with Jesus the Galilean.' 70. *But he denied it before them all, saying, 'I do not know what you mean.'* 71. *And when he went out to the entrance, another servant girl saw him, and she said to the bystanders, 'This man was with Jesus of Nazareth.'* 72. *And again he denied it with an oath: 'I do not know the man.'*

73. *After a little while the bystanders came up and said to Peter, 'Certainly you too are one of them, for your accent betrays you.'* 74. *Then he began to invoke a curse on himself and to swear, 'I do not know the man.' And immediately the rooster crowed.* 75. *And Peter remembered the saying of Jesus, 'Before the rooster crows, you will deny me three times.' And he went out and wept bitterly.*

One can only imagine Peter's shame when he realized what he had done. Now, some will say that he deserves death for betraying the Son of Man, especially in light of Jesus's words in **Matthew 10:33**, "*...but whoever denies me before men, I also will deny before my Father who is in heaven.*" At first glance, it would appear that Peter's denial of Jesus would be returned in kind by the Savior, but that is not the case, thankfully. You see, the **Matthew 10:33** verse speaks of a total denial of Jesus, not one born from a brief moment of fear. What is of interest to us is that besides the shame he must have felt, we know of no other consequence of his lying, at least not as it relates to direct punishment from God.

Lastly, when we leave the confines of the church building and act like the world for the rest of the week, are we not lying about who we are? Or worse, are we lying about who we are when we are at church? We should never deny Jesus, but if we do so to preserve our life and repent thereof, like Peter, we can find forgiveness.

Chapter 18
Ananias and Sapphira (Act. 5)

Imagine if one lie could end your life instantly. No chance to beg for forgiveness, no chance to repent, no chance to fix the mistake, just immediate death. Well, that happened to a couple in the New Testament. Let's read the story of Ananias and Sapphira in **Acts 5:1-11**,

But a man named Ananias, with his wife Sapphira, sold a piece of property, 2. and with his wife's knowledge he kept back for himself some of the proceeds and brought only a part of it and laid it at the apostles' feet. 3. But Peter said, 'Ananias, why has Satan filled your heart to lie to the Holy Spirit and to keep back for yourself part of the proceeds of the land? 4. While it remained unsold, did it not remain your own? And after it was sold, was it not at your disposal? Why is it that you have contrived this deed in your heart? You have not lied to man but to God.'

5. When Ananias heard these words, he fell down and breathed his last. And great fear came upon all who heard of it. 6. The young men rose and wrapped him up and carried him out and buried him. 7. After an interval of about three hours his wife came in, not knowing what had happened. 8. And Peter said to her, 'Tell me whether you sold the land for so much.' And she said, 'Yes, for so much.' 9. But Peter said to her, 'How is it that you have agreed together to test the Spirit of the Lord? Behold, the feet of those who have buried your husband are at the door, and they will carry you out.' 10. Immediately she fell down at his feet and breathed her last. When the young men came in they

found her dead, and they carried her out and buried her beside
her husband. ¹¹· And great fear came upon the whole church and
upon all who heard of these things.

Many people who read this story may feel like it was unfair that they were not given a chance to fix their lies. Admittedly, it seems rather a harsh punishment for keeping some of the money for themselves. One would even be forgiven for thinking they probably needed it to survive. Why would they have to give everything to the apostles only to be destitute and starve? Would it not make perfect sense to give what they could and keep some for themselves? To understand why the punishment was so immediate and extreme, we must understand the context in which it occurred. At the time it happened, the church was in its infancy years, and any contradiction would subvert its impact on the greater community.

The communal unity spoken of in **Acts 4:32** was being harmed and had to be rectified in a way that clearly sent a message to the church as well as the community – Christ would not allow His church to be stained by the action of man. This is clearly illustrated in the words of the last verse: "*And great fear came upon the whole church and upon all who heard of these things.*" God's judgment may not be instantaneous anymore (for the most part), but that does not mean a price for our dishonesty will not be exacted. The passage is a sobering reminder of the need for the community, and by extension, us, to be honest in all our dealings, but even more so when it comes to the church.

Chapter 19
Midwives Lie to Pharaoh (Exo. 1)

The following two chapters will be quite a turn-around in God's treatment of liars. In the first chapter of the book of Exodus, the reigning Pharaoh at the time became concerned about the growing Hebrew population: *"Now there arose a new king over Egypt, who did not know Joseph. ⁹· And he said to his people, "Behold, the people of Israel are too many and too mighty for us"* (**Exodus 1:8-9**). In v.10, we are told that he feared the subjugated Jews would join Egypt's enemies in the event of a war and help overthrow them. He then came up with what he thought was an ingenious plan, but even that failed. **Exodus 1:11-12**,

> *Therefore they set taskmasters over them to afflict them with heavy burdens. They built for Pharaoh store cities, Pithom and Raamses. ¹²· But the more they were oppressed, the more they multiplied and the more they spread abroad. And the Egyptians were in dread of the people of Israel.*

Ultimately, the Pharaoh decided on an even more evil plan to keep the Hebrew population under control. **Exodus 1:15-16**,

> *Then the king of Egypt said to the Hebrew midwives, one of whom was named Shiphrah and the other Puah, ¹⁶· 'When you serve as midwife to the Hebrew women and see them on the birthstool, if it is a son, you shall kill him, but if it is a daughter, she shall live.'*

It is hard to imagine that someone could be so afraid of a nation that he would resort to attempted infanticide.

While he must have congratulated himself on his brilliant plan to curtail the growth of his slave nation, he overlooked one very important point, which is illustrated by Exodus 1:17, "*But the midwives feared God and did not do as the king of Egypt commanded them, but let the male children live*" They feared God more than they feared the king, so they refused to obey him, but obviously at some point he was going to notice lots of baby boys were being born and know that they had not listened to him. That did indeed happen, and when he called them to answer for their apparent disobedience, they smartly replied with the words of **Exodus 1:19**, "*The midwives said to Pharaoh, 'Because the Hebrew women are not like the Egyptian women, for they are vigorous and give birth before the midwife comes to them.'*"

As brave as they were to go against the Pharaoh and risk possible death, they still lied to him, and we know God does not tolerate lies. That said, what He does may surprise us and is the focus of this chapter. **Exodus 1:20-21**, "*So God dealt well with the midwives. And the people multiplied and grew very strong. 21. And because the midwives feared God, he gave them families.*" Strangely, the God who hates lies and cannot Himself lie not only tolerated their lies but even went so far as to bless them with families and children of their own. At this point, I will continue with the next chapter so that I can deal with the explanation of both cases at once.

Chapter 20

Rahab Lies to the King's Men (Jos. 2)

In **Joshua 2:1**, Joshua sends out two spies to Jericho, where they end up lodging at the home of Rahab, who was a prostitute. After the king of Jericho is told they are there, Rahab blatantly lies to him: **Joshua 2:3-5**,

> *Then the king of Jericho sent to Rahab, saying, 'Bring out the men who have come to you, who entered your house, for they have come to search out all the land.' 4. But the woman had taken the two men and hidden them. And she said, 'True, the men came to me, but I did not know where they were from. 5. And when the gate was about to be closed at dark, the men went out. I do not know where the men went. Pursue them quickly, for you will overtake them.'*

Whenever I read this story, and especially the last verse, I imagine in my mind's eye the soldiers racing out of the city, trying to find the spies. They chased the "ghost spies" for three days until they reached the fords, but they still did not see them. How their moods must have dropped when they realized the spies had escaped. In the meantime, Rahab confessed her faith in the Lord and asked them (the spies) to save her and her family when they destroyed Jericho. Fast forward to chapter six and the destruction of Jericho, and we find that Rahab and her family were indeed saved.

Joshua 6:16-17,

> *And at the seventh time, when the priests had blown the trumpets, Joshua said to the people, 'Shout, for the Lord has given you the city. 17. And the city and all that is within it shall be devoted to the Lord for destruction. Only Rahab the prostitute*

and all who are with her in her house shall live, because she hid the messengers whom we sent.'

Not only is she and her entire family and everyone connected to them saved, but she is also integrated into the Jewish community: **Joshua 6:25,**

But Rahab the prostitute and her father's household and all who belonged to her, Joshua saved alive. And she has lived in Israel to this day, because she hid the messengers whom Joshua sent to spy out Jericho.

So, what do the midwives and Rahab have in common? The God of the universe, who cannot lie and hates lies, not only didn't punish them for their lies but even went as far as to reward them. So, the obvious question is, "Why would God reward some liars and kill others?" In a previous chapter, we have explained why he killed Ananias and Sapphira, so let's deal with why He rewarded those in question. God is a just and fair God, so He will not punish us when we are forced to lie to save someone. Their lies were not for their benefit or for the material benefit of others but rather a necessity to save the lives of innocent babies and people that Joshua had sent to spy on Jericho.

Chapter 21
The Impact and Danger of Lying

As we have seen from all our examples, lying has an impact. No one can deny the destructive nature of lies. They range from relatively harmless "white" lies to ones that are so destructive that they literally changed the course of history. Their effects can be devastating. Many people have found them so disturbing and disruptive that they could not live with the consequences and chose to end their lives instead. When someone lies about us, we take it personally, and who would blame us? I bet it would not take more than a second for you to think about a time when someone's lies about you caused you anywhere from mild to significant discomfort.

Lies can end careers, marriages, friendships, and even family bonds. Just after we came to live in the United States, we met a cowboy who was working on the ranch where we had briefly stayed. He was going through an absolutely horrid time. Accused of sexually inappropriate contact by his daughter and her best friend, he was labeled as a sex offender. The problem was that both girls admitted that his strict parenting style drove them to concoct the story of their abuse. Even after they came forward and admitted to the deception, it took three years for the state to conclude that the girls had indeed lied.

Their lies cost him his wife, his relationship with his family, his job as a school administrator, and many friends. Additionally, it took five long years for him to be removed from the sex offender registry. The girls had not thought about the devastation their lies would cause. It did not matter to them that he had lost his wife, his job, his friends, and even his honor because liars like them are self-centered. As long as they get what they want, they could care less for anything or anyone else.

Chapter 22
Why Do We Lie?

Why we lie is an interesting question, and I am positive there are more reasons than I can come up with in this chapter, but I will look at some of the more common ones. I will list them in no particular order. The first one is to protect oneself. I suppose it can be termed self-preservation, but I am careful of that because there are degrees associated with that term. Let me explain. When someone physically threatens your life and the only way to save yourself is to lie, that is the highest degree of self-preservation.

An example would be if someone points a gun at you and demands to know if you slept with his girlfriend, you would lie, even if you had (To be clear, I am not condoning that behavior but instead just giving an extreme example of self-preservation). A lie that warrants a less extreme lie for self-preservation probably happened to you many times in your life. A parent asks you if you did this or that, and knowing that you did, you choose to lie to escape the consequences of your action. Be truthful, and you lose privileges like your cell phone or being able to go out. Lie, and you may get away with it.

The second reason seems far more innocent. In fact, it could even be seen as honorable or heroic. It is the lie we tell to protect someone from harm. Remember, in the first instance, we lied to protect ourselves, but now we are lying to protect someone else. A rather extreme example would be if a man were looking to beat up another person and we lied about the victim's whereabouts. This type of untruthfulness is also used to spare someone's feelings. An example is when a child shows you a self-portrait that looks more like a scrambled mess than them, we lie and tell them it is beautiful. Similarly, when a friend asks us if we think they are ugly, we may think that to ourselves, but we tell them they are good-looking to spare their feelings. I am sure you can think of many more examples of lying to protect someone, so let's move on.

A third reason we lie is to impress others. We may have low self-esteem and tell fanciful, made-up stories that embellish our unimpressive accomplishments in life. We may even lie outright about some heroic action we took – all to impress someone. People who indulge in these types of lies run the risk of beginning to believe the lies they tell and will embellish old stories even more as time goes on. For example, a college student who never played football claims that he was a star player to impress a girl he has his eye on. Sad as it is, it does not excuse the lie, and being honest about who you are is more important than trying to impress other people. People who tell these lies fail to realize that God loves them as they are, and they should be happy with that.

A fourth reason for lying is when someone is trying to hide a traumatic event. It is similar to the self-preservation lie but more psychological than that one. Take, for example, when an adult abuses a child. The child may find the abuse so traumatic that they lie to others and even themselves by saying it never happened. This also is the case in many homes where one spouse abuses the other, but when confronted by friends and family, they lie and say everything is okay. We have all seen film clips or even experienced a woman blaming a black eye on accidentally walking into a door instead of admitting it was her husband.

If it is motivated by fear of harm, it naturally falls into the self-preservation category, but when it is to protect their Psyche, it falls into this one. Unfortunately, they live lying about something they should take care of. A fifth reason is that someone is a compulsive or pathological liar. This person cannot help themselves and has no apparent reason for lying. Almost everything they say is a lie, at least partly so, and they feel no guilt when doing so. The danger they face is that they will eventually begin to believe their lies, and then the difference between the lie and reality will be blurred. These liars often concoct elaborate lies and usually cannot help themselves. Certain personality disorders are associated with pathological lying, such as narcissism or antisocial personality disorder.

I could write a lot more about the different reasons for lying, but for the sake of brevity, I will only mention a few more before moving on to the next chapter. There are lies to impress at work to get an increase, lies for pleasure, as in besmearing someone's character for fun, and lies to keep secrets. That last reason for lying could include lying about bad habits like using drugs or looking at pornography. Whatever the reason, lying will erode trust in relationships and may negatively affect the person's psychological well-being. If you tend to be untruthful, I seriously urge you to do some honest self-reflection and take steps to correct your behavior. You may need to speak to someone you trust or a professional counselor with the experience to help you navigate your way back to a more truthful existence.

Chapter 23
Those "White" Lies

There are lies we have grown up with and lies we tell for the same reasons. But before delving into some of them, here is a thought to ponder as you read the rest of the chapter. Do you realize that the lies we will speak of literally teach our children that lying is okay? We lie to them most of their early childhood and then say things like, "If there is one thing I will not tolerate in this house, it is lying. I literally hate lies, and I better never catch you lying to me, or you will suffer the consequences." Just keep that in mind as you continue reading.

We have many white lies, but here is a selection of the most common ones. The first is, of course, Santa Claus. We tell children that a large man in a red suit flies worldwide in a sled in one night, navigates down chimneys, and leaves presents under the Christmas tree. We also tell them that little elves make all the presents. Next, we have the Easter Bunny. This character hides Easter eggs with candies and other goodies in them for the children to find. The fact that it takes away from the real reason we celebrate Easter should be concerning. We also have the tooth fairy, which is a personal peeve of mine. This fairy uses dirty, old, broken, and maybe stinky teeth to build a house. Talk about an unhygienic house.

I remember as a child when a favorite dog of mine was suddenly not around anymore. My parents told me he went to live on the farm with the other dogs. Strangely, my pet goldfish also decided randomly one day to go to the ocean to be with his family, probably by way of the toilet bowl. We also tell them babies are delivered by a stork and unicorns are real (technically, unicorns are, though, since one-horned rhinos were termed that previously). Here are my thoughts on the matter. Wouldn't it be okay if we didn't tell our children about Santa and still gave them presents? Also, we could hide the Easter eggs and not lie and say some super intelligent bunny did it. And, the one that would make me most happy: we could just give the kiddos a dollar or whatever for a tooth that fell out. I know people will undoubtedly say it is all about the magic of being a child, but is it? Are we teaching them to lie from the time they are babies while expecting them not to lie to us EVER?

Chapter 24
So, Is There a Time I Can Lie?

The easy answer is "No!" but life is much more complicated than that. The goal should always be never to lie. Let's refresh our memories about what God thinks of lying: **Proverbs 6:16-19,**

> *There are six things that the Lord hates, seven that are an abomination to him:* [17.] *haughty eyes, a lying tongue, and hands that shed innocent blood,* [18.] *a heart that devises wicked plans, feet that make haste to run to evil,* [19.] *a false witness who breathes out lies, and one who sows discord among brothers.*

And let's also refresh our memories about the ultimate consequences of lying, which is undoubtedly the most common sin: **Romans 6:23,** *"For the wages of sin is death..."*

God hates sin, lying is sin, and the wages of sin is death – pretty clear, I would say, but as I mentioned at the start of the chapter and as we discovered in earlier ones, life is not always black and white. Moreover, some people who did not lie to save a human life also seemed to benefit from their sinful actions. Before I answer that, I want to draw your attention to one of my favorite verses in the Bible: *"For my thoughts are not your thoughts, neither are your ways my ways, declares the Lord.* [9.] *For as the heavens are higher than the earth, so are my ways higher than your ways and my thoughts than your thoughts"* (**Isaiah 55:8-9**). From that scripture, it is clear that there are some things we cannot explain, but that does not mean we cannot find a reasonable explanation for mysteries like the one currently under question.

We know lying to save someone's life is justifiable, but there is another reason that a lie will not be held against man. That reason has to do with the greater plan of God, like in the case of Jacob lying to Isaac. That lie was part of the unfolding of God's plan for Israel, but we should not take it for granted that no punishment was metered out by God. Again, taking the case of Jacob as an example, we see that he had both personal and family problems.

Personally, he had to flee from his home, lived in fear of Esau's retaliation for years, and experienced deceit himself at the hands of his uncle Laban. His family was also fraught with conflict, and he struggled with issues among his wives and children. Was this as a direct result of the lie? We do not know, but in the same breath, we cannot say it wasn't. Let's, instead, concentrate on trying not to lie rather than concerning ourselves with what happened to those who did and seemingly were not punished.

Chapter 25
Fighting the Urge to Lie

Anyone who does not have an underlying psychological condition that precipitates this type of behavior can stop lying. But let's also be clear in stating that no one can stop lying altogether. That is just an unfortunate byproduct of not being divine. Also, do not fool yourself into thinking it will be as easy as saying, "I will never lie again!" It will take hard work and much perseverance to go from being a habitual liar to someone who only lies occasionally. By the way, it is not only habitual liars who should work on stopping that behavior, but all of us.

We all lie more than we should. **Proverbs 12:19**, "*Truthful lips endure forever, but a lying tongue is but for a moment.*" If you are the worst kind of liar, the habitual liar who has been doing this for a long time and actually believes some of your lies, you must take action. You should immediately contact a professional counselor to help you stop that destructive behavior. Thinking that you can do it alone or that a family member or friend can help you dramatically increases the risk of failure. Find a professional and be totally honest with them. If you are not a habitual liar but find yourself lying more than you would like to, it may be sufficient for you to confide in a trusted family member, friend, or church leader.

Make sure it is someone you trust who will not divulge your secret to others. An accountability partner will go a long way to help you overcome your weakness of being untruthful. If you are someone a liar has trusted enough to confide in, be respectful and never break their trust in you. They did not come and bear their hearts to you just so that you can tell your spouse, best friend(s), or anyone else for that fact. Too many people have had their trust shattered by someone who may not be inclined to lie but is a serious gossiper.

If you are wary of letting others know for fear of them betraying your secret and you cannot afford a counselor, some pastoral counselors offer their services for free. You can also find books in stores, libraries, and online. But above all, immerse yourself in the Bible, attend a faithful congregation, and pray, pray, pray. Formulate a plan to rid yourself of this weakness. Be patient, persevere, and again, above all else, pray. And always remember **Philippians 4:13**, *"I can do all things through him who strengthens me."*

Chapter 26

Is the Sin of Lying Forgivable

If you have read the entire book, I think the answer is already apparent to you, but if you have not, the answer is an emphatic "Yes!" In fact, the only sin that is not forgivable is mentioned in **Matthew 12:31-32**,

> *Therefore I tell you, every sin and blasphemy will be forgiven people, but the blasphemy against the Spirit will not be forgiven.*
> 32. *And whoever speaks a word against the Son of Man will be forgiven, but whoever speaks against the Holy Spirit will not be forgiven, either in this age or in the age to come.*

Any explanation of those verses is beyond the scope of this book, but suffice it to say that lying does not fall into that category of sin. Lying can and will be forgiven if the perpetrator is genuinely repentant of their untruthfulness: "*If we confess our sins, he is faithful and just to forgive us our sins and to cleanse us from all unrighteousness*" (**1 John 1:9**). We are a fallen people, and we will stumble occasionally, but God, who is just and gracious in His mercy, will forgive us of our trespasses. Obviously, I am not condoning lying.

We should never lie frivolously because of the dangers associated with it, and, more importantly, God disapproves of it. That said, if circumstances force us to lie, we must understand that it is not an automatic "Go to hell" judgment. If you find yourself lying more than you ought to, I urge you to find professional help before it is too late. Don't be afraid to ask for help, and don't forget to study your Bible and pray.